THE BUBBA HANDBOOK

An Insider's Guide to the Bubba Way of Life

The Editors of *Bubba Magazine*

A Perigee Book

To Bill

Perigee Books
are published by
The Putnam Publishing Group
200 Madison Avenue
New York, NY 10016

ISBN 0-399-51850-9

Cover illustration © 1993 by Bay Rigby

Printed in the United States of America

1 2 3 4 5 6 7 8 9 10

For *Bubba Magazine* product
information call the Bubba Hotline
at 800-57-BUBBA.

THE BUBBA HANDBOOK

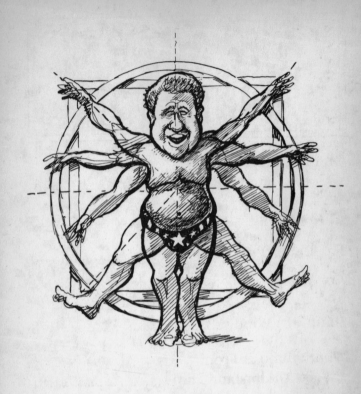

On the 13th Day, God Created Bubba?

Actually, God didn't create Bubba until about 1950. But guys like Achilles, Davy Crockett, and Theodore Roosevelt had Bubba characteristics. After pounding a few Trojans, Achilles would have loved to grab a cold one and click from college football to old Cagney movies—if he could have.

But that's the point. Sure, the American frontier experience was a major ingredient in the Bubba formula. So was fighting Trojans, lions, and dinosaurs, for that matter. And, granted, beer had been around since the first good ol' Egyptian brewed up a vat of grain back in 8000 B.C. But for Bubba to *be*, several refinements in living conditions had to occur.

Preparation "H" (High Gear)

Bubba's primordial elements began to coalesce around the turn of the century. First the air conditioner was invented in 1902. Next,

that nutritional staple the Moon Pie was born in a Chattanooga bakery in 1918. And the first upholstered La-Z-Boy recliner rolled off the production line in 1929. Now you're talking.

Then, in swift succession, the first drive-in movie theater opened (1933), canned beer went on sale (1935), the first TV (a cartoon of Felix the Cat) hit the airwaves, and McDonald's fried up its first patty (1937). The elements were clearly aligning to create the Cradle of Bubba Civilization. In anticipation, Sam Walton even opened his first retail outlet (1945).

The Bubba Big Bang

It must have occurred on a rowdy Saturday night during the keg party of all keg parties. Few probably noticed, and even fewer still could have predicted that from it would be born the flip-top beer can, a plague of Labrador retrievers, and a President from Arkansas.

The most probable year was 1950—the year the All America Football Conference

THE BUBBA YEARS

1950—John Wayne makes *The Sands of Iwo Jima.* The first Bubba decade begins.

1954—McDonald's bought by Ray Crock.

1956—Elvis stars in *Love Me Tender.*

merged with the NFL, starting the league's rise to stardom. The year Ford introduced the F-100 pickup truck with the slogan "Where men are men, and trucks are Ford V-8s." And the year *The Sands of Iwo Jima* was released, starring a guy named John Wayne.

While scholars are still debating the exact date and cause of the Bubba Big Bang, one thing is certain: Bubba had arrived. Soon he was towing home a rented big tank grill for his annual cookout party, and no good bass-fishing lake was too far for him to reach, bass boat hitched behind pickup. With color TV and pro football, Bubba communed with fellow males on Sunday, and if he needed more, he did it again on Monday night. Beer became the national beverage.

In fact, scholars have proposed many theories linking beer to Bubba's Creation. Consider these relationships from the formative years: Moon Pies (great with beer), recliner (great place to drink a cold one), drive-in

---

1957—Patsy Cline wins the Arthur Godfrey Talent Scouts contest with hit "Walkin' After Midnight."

1958—Robert Mitchum revs across big screen in *Thunder Road*, original Bubba car-chase flick.

1959—Chevrolet introduces the El Camino. Bubba can drive to work and haul manure in the same car.

movie (great place to take a coolerfull), pickup truck (perfect for hauling kegs)...Hmmm.

Whatever the connection, the Bubba creature quickly showed a hearty appetite, a propensity to laugh, an innate sense for work efficiency, and even a tendency to sentimentality—at times "The Star-Spangled Banner" could bring tears to his eyes.

The Aftermath

By 1977, Bubba had made it to the White House—through the back door. While Jimmy had the nation sweating like a glass of iced tea on a Georgia summer day, Billy—the patron saint of Bubbas—introduced the world to Billy Beer. Soon the stage was set for cable television, the remote control, and a First Mom named Virginia Cassidy Blythe Clinton Dwire Kelly—the mother of all Bubbettes.

Which brings us to Bubba's zenith. The headlines read "Hubba Bubba!" when the Double-Bubba ticket triumphed in '92. Five

»

1960—*The Andy Griffith Show* premieres on CBS.

1962—Easy-open beer can test-marketed. Bubba chucks his can opener.

1964—First Ford Mustang rolls off assembly line.

1965—First commercial satellite TV.

1971—Colts draft Bubba Smith in first round.

hundred cable channels are on the way. Duck season will be here again before too long. Bubba feels good. He is gaining on his ultimate goal: Satisfaction. □

1972—Dallas Cowboys hire the Cowgirls, seven scantily clad dancers.

1974—Energy crisis leads to CB boom. "Good buddy" becomes popular salutation.

1977—Bubba gets a taste of Billy Beer.

1979—John Madden finds his true calling—on TV.

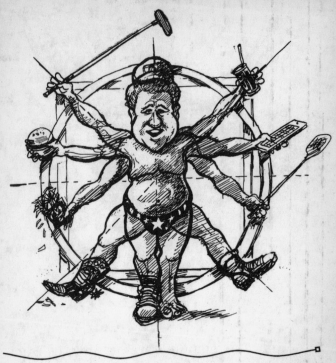

1979—*Dukes of Hazzard* premieres. Good ol' southern family fights for "truth, justice, and wild driving."

1982—After 323 victories, Bear Bryant retires.

1983—B. A. Baracus (a.k.a. Mr. T) debuts on *The A-Team.* "You betta watch out, sucka!" widely quoted.

1984—Merle Haggard buys a round for the patrons of Billy Bob's in Fort Worth—all 5,095 of them.

1991—Dr. Pepper museum opens in Waco.

1993—The Bubbadent inaugurated in DC. *Bubba Magazine* is born.

Are You a Bubba?

The Basic Bubba Quiz

If you are unsure whether you're a Bubba (or a Bubbette, as the case may be), take this test, keep score, and don't cheat. At the end, find the range in which your total score falls and read how you rated. If you score 150 or above, turn to page 88, and try your hand at the BubbaMaster Quiz. If you already know you're a Bubba, just git on back there.

Give yourself 10 points for each correct answer:

1. *"Y'all" refers to*
    a. one person
    b. more than one person
    c. one or more people
    d. a small sailing ship

2. *"Barbecue" refers to*
   a. weenies on the backyard grill
   b. the backyard grill itself
   c. the spare ribs over at the Polynesian Delight on Rte. 9
   d. slow-cooked pork or beef in a sauce whose ingredients you wouldn't reveal to a dying friend

3. *They don't smoke _____ in Muskogee.*
   a. aardvarks
   b. corncob pipes
   c. Mary Jane
   d. cowpies

4. *A corn dog is*
   a. a painful foot condition
   b. a farm animal
   c. a hot dog wrapped in cornbread and deep-fried
   d. a pet trained by moonshiners to watch for revenue agents

5. *French impressionistic composer Maurice Ravel composed which ballet in 1912?*
   a. *Daphnis et Chloe*
   b. *Daphnis et Camille*
   c. *Dance of the Tartar Sauce Eaters*
   d. Maurice who?

6. *What Philadelphia Eagles linebacker knocked New York Giants golden-boy running back and future Cody-dad Frank Gifford senseless in a 1960 NFL game?*

    a. Chuck Rednarik

    b. Chuck E. Cheese

    c. Bronco Nagurski

    d. Zeke Bratkowski

7. *What Bubba Hall of Fame movie star wisely jettisoned his real first name, Marion?*

    a. George Kennedy   c. Roseanne Barr

    b. John Wayne   d. James Cagney

8. *Every now and then even a blind hog finds*
    a. an apple   c. his way home
    b. an acorn   d. another blind hog

9. *For a hot date you deck yourself out in*
    a. an Armani suit
    b. bikini underwear
    c. cologne with a French name
    d. a clean pair of Dickies

10. *You can get really worked up for a debate over*
    a. realism versus romanticism
    b. collectivism versus objectivism
    c. modernism versus classicism
    d. presoaked charcoal versus regular

11. *The wife and kids are in the car and Grandma's Sunday dinner starts in five minutes. You realize there's a small hole in your oil pan. What do you do?*
    a. Call a wrecker
    b. Tell Granny you can't make it, and weld an old paint can over the hole
    c. Go for it
    d. Patch the hole with duct tape

12. *Hegel is to Kant as Nietzsche is to*
    a. Spinoza
    b. a cold six of Bud
    c. Comte
    d. Plato

13. *Bubba marvels at human ingenuity every time he thinks of*
    a. the polio vaccine
    b. the space program
    c. the theory of relativity
    d. Slim Jim meat snacks

14. *When a mountain Bubba tells you he spent last Sunday "sangin'," it most likely means he*
    a. is a member of the church choir
    b. gave blood
    c. has a sack of freshly dug ginseng hid somewhere
    d. plays the banjo

15. *Bubba says it's not the heat, it's*
    a. the humidity
    b. the rain
    c. the snow
    d. oh hell, it is so the heat

16. *The picturesque town of Staunton, Virginia, produced which Bubba Hall of Fame country group?*

    a. The Osborne Brothers

    b. The Statler Brothers

    c. Dr. Joyce Brothers

    d. Flatt & Scruggs

17. *Sure, Paris has the* Mona Lisa, *but if you want your picture taken next to Buford Pusser's Death Car, you'll have to visit*

    a. Pigeon Forge, Tennessee

    b. Cape May, New Jersey

    c. Universal Studios

    d. Owensboro, Kentucky

18. *Since it's the last American-owned manufacturer of televisions, chances are you'll find Bubba resting his weary bones in front of*

    a. an RCA

    b. a Zenith

    c. a Magnavox

    d. There are no more American-owned manufacturers

19. *Which disease is most commonly suffered by Bubbas?*

a. seborrhea

b. psoriasis

c. tapeworms

d. dunlop disease

20. *Modern architecture really begins with the introduction of*

a. the cantilever

b. steel-frame construction

c. the prairie style

d. the cinder block

Extra Credit. *Asked how he captured 132 German soldiers all by himself during a World War I battle, Alvin York of Fentress County, Tennessee, told his commanding officer:*

a. "I can shoot the left eye off a tick at fifty yards."

b. "Weren't nothin' to it."

c. "I surrounded 'em."

d. "Jes' lucky, I reckon."

Basic Bubba Quiz Answers

1-b. Faux-Bubba urban cowboys who say "How y'all doin'?" or "Where y'all going?" to one person are full of mechanical bull. It's strictly plural.

2-d. "Barbecue" and "grilling" should not be confused.

3-c. Mary Jane. Actually marijuana, as in the Haggard tune.

4-c. Proving once again that a little cornmeal and hot grease can make anything taste better.

5-d. Bubba has been to the ballet only once, and that was by mistake. He thought *The Nutcracker* was a kung fu movie. If you actually knew that Ravel wrote *Daphnis et Chloe*, subtract 10 points from your score. *We* looked it up.

6-a. Next play: Off-tackle to Kathy Lee.

7-b. *True Grit*, starring Marion Michael Morrison. It just wouldn't sound right.

8-b. Bubba doesn't mind praise for his accomplishments, he just can't stand talking about them himself. This is his stock explanation for a personal success.

9-d. America's most venerable Bubba outfitter—for work or play.

10-d. Some guys prefer the convenience of charcoal presoaked in lighter fluid. But Bubba traditionalists still like the way a can of liquid fire at their side makes them feel.

11-d. Bubba doesn't want to miss Grandma's pork chops, so he quick-fixes it with duct tape and welds the paint can in later.

12-b. When in doubt, choose beer.

13-d. Spicy, compact, Bubbalicious.

14-c. Bubba doesn't hold much with the mystical powers of ginseng, or "'sang," but Asians paying up to $200 a pound for something that grows wild in the woods is all the mysticism he needs.

15-d. Let's settle this once and for all. It's the HEAT. When was the last time you started a fire with a wet rag?

16-b. "Movies are great medicine/Thank you, Thomas Edison/For giving us the best years of our lives."

17-a. Don't forget to stop in and say "Hey" to Miss Parton just down the road at Dollywood.

18-b. If Zenith bails out, Bubba may have to go back to rockin' on the front porch.

19-d. It means his belly done lopped over his belt.

20-d. Versatile, inexpensive, and there are a thousand uses for the leftover ones. Ever tried to prop up an old Chevy with a cantilever?

Extra Credit-c. Only a Bubba demigod such as Sgt. York could report in all seriousness and humility that he "surrounded" 132 men. A crack shot, York had the hapless Huns thinking he was a dozen or more well-armed Americans. If you ask Bubba, they were right.

Determining Your B.Q. (Bubba Quotient)

Give yourself 10 points for each correct answer. Add up your score, and tack on 5 points if you didn't ask anyone for help.

0-50: Not a Bubba

You're not even comfortable with the concept. Right now you're worried that if someone sees you holding this book they'll think you're insensitive.

50-100: Bubba Wannabe

You think you might like to be a Bubba, but when you try to act or dress like one you look like a pullout from the Eddie Bauer catalogue. You considered *Iron John* a provocative book.

100-150: B.I.T. (Bubba-In-Training)

You've made several Bubba friends and they seem to like you. At least they don't seem to dislike you. For now, you're content to stay quiet and study their habits.

150-210: Bubba

You may, repeat, *may*, just qualify. To see if you do, move on to the BubbaMaster Quiz on page 88.

The Bubba Barometer

There are two ways to construct an accurate forecast of how the Bubbadent will manage the country. One is to read all of his speeches and policy statements, analyze the Cabinet selections until you're blue in the face, and subject the man to a battery of personality tests at some institute in Switzerland. The other is to monitor the behavior of the nearest Bubba and do some simple extrapolation:

Observation: Bubba's wife needs to run into the mall for "just two minutes," and even though it always takes an hour, Bubba sits with the car running in the loading zone.
Conclusion: President Clinton will be overly optimistic when sending legislation to Congress.

Observation: Bubba, feeling around under the seat of his car for the boiled peanut he just dropped, finds the copy of *Action Jackson* he rented two weeks ago. He goes to the video store and considers sticking the tape in the after-hours slot and running. But, overcome by conscience, he finally goes inside and sheepishly pays the $28 he owes them.

Conclusion: President Clinton will tackle the federal deficit.

Observation: Bubba endears himself to the waitress at the local Mexican restaurant by repeatedly yelling out the three phrases he remembers from eighth-grade Spanish class.

Conclusion: President Clinton will achieve an easy rapport with foreign dignitaries.

———————

Observation: Bubba watches a pro golf match on TV and hollers enthusiastically when Curtis Strange sinks a two-foot putt for par.
Conclusion: President Clinton will actually enjoy attending those 16-hour budget sessions.

———————

Observation: Bubba sees a man throw a Pepsi can onto the side of the road. Bubba pulls up beside the man at the next red light, honks his horn, and delivers a loud critique of his mother's child-rearing abilities.
Conclusion: Bill Clinton will expand the powers of the E.P.A.

———————

Observation: Bubba's wife's car has an ignition problem. She calls AAA. Bubba calls AAA back, tells them not to come, and gets under the hood himself. An hour later, the car needs a new ignition, a new alternator, and a valve job.
Conclusion: President Clinton will drastically reduce the size of the White House staff. He will later quietly increase the size of the White House staff.

Observation: After a year of traditional grooming, the White House lawn starts to accumulate grilling equipment, lawn and garden tools, sporting goods, and car parts.

Conclusion: The Bubbadent feels at home. Plans to stay for eight years.

THE BUBBA PRIMER

PRIMER

Bubba A to Z

Ace: Popular Bubba nickname—along with Booger, Buddy, Buster, Cooter, Doc, Dude, Hawk, Hoss, Hot Rod, Junior, Rusty, Shorty, Skeeter, Slick, Slim, Snake, and Stump.

Joe Alexander: Set the bareback-bull-riding record atop Sippin' Velvet at the Cheyenne Rodeo in '74. Not your average Joe.

Amarillo: Every cross-country trucker must stop in at Amarillo's Big Texan Steak Ranch on Rte. 40 to have a go at their 72-ounce steak. If you can eat one in 45 minutes—it's free.

America's Team: With moves like the double axe handle and the camel clutch, Heidi Lee Morgan and Misty Blue, better known as Team America, captured the L.P.W.A. World Tag Team Title belt and the hearts of their fans.

And you thought America's Team was the Cowboys.

All About Varmint Hunting: Classic Bubba lit by Nick Sisley. Consider this sentence: "Starlings, those dastardly birds brought over from Europe, are the nation's most underrated, underharvested, and underutilized varmint." Why did he write the book? "Varmint hunting and varmint hunters have been cheated through the history of outdoor literature."

Bacon?: Yes, please.

Badges?: "We don't need no steenkin' badges." Perhaps the best line Bogart ever had to endure. Bubba can make this oft-repeated Q&A last an eternity.

Bait shop: Where Bubba gets crawlers, daredevils, and uncluttered politics, all in one stop.

Barbershop: While many of his friends swear by the Hair Cuttery at the mall, Bubba sticks to the barbershop his father took him to when he was a kid. There are few feelings in life better than a straight-razor neck shave with warm shaving cream. (See also *Penthouse*.)

Bar code: Shirts and shoes required.

Bass boat: Why Bubba doesn't own his house.

B.C. Powder: Most Bubbas use headache powders like Goody's, B.C., and Stanback. Bubba prefers powder to pills. He says it works better, but he's really been hit by the powder ads, which frequently appear during country-music shows and NASCAR races.

Beer joint: It's not fancy, but Bubba's credit is good, and the gang's always there. When he comes in, this is what you hear: "Hey, Bubba." "Hey, Bubba." "Hey, Bubba." "Hey, Bubba."

Belt buckle: Behind Bubba's paunch, his brass resume features the logo of his favorite beer, a soaring eagle, or an entire scene involving a duck blind. Read the hand-tooled belt strap for Bubba's nickname, and sometimes his gal's, usually embossed in block letters.

Billy: If you have to ask "Billy WHO?" deduct 10 points from your "Are You a Bubba?" score. Hint: He had his own beer. His brother was named Jimmy. And he ate a lot of boiled peanuts. He is the patron saint of all Bubbas.

Bloodworms: Bubba's favorite surf-casting bait. To keep 'em fresh, he hides them in the fridge behind the pickles.

Bore: The width of a shotgun or rifle barrel. Also, Aunt Esther at suppertime.

Boss Hogg: Big trouble for the Duke brothers. Why Bubba never wears a white flannel suit.

Bowling shirt: By nature, devoid of natural fibers. The collar is broad and floppy, the buttons go all the way down, and Bubba's name in flowing script is obligatory on the back or breast pocket. Always short-sleeved.

Box scores: Why Bubba spends so much time

in the bathroom with the sports page.

Broccoli: As in Albert Broccoli, Bond producer. Bubba was offended by the names of Bond's babes—Dr. Goodhead, Pussy Galore, Octopussy. Right. He's seen parts of all of 'em a hundred times.

Brother-in-law: Every Bubba can only hope that his brother-in-law is a Bubba, and they tend to be. For the rest of his life, this is the guy Bubba has to look at during Thanksgiving dinner and stand next to at 5:30 A.M. in the duck blind. Suffice it to say that if bro-in-law is a dingleberry, there's gonna be hell to pay.

Brunswick stew: Ruritan Club fundraiser staple, once made with squirrel and rabbit in large black kettles. Southern TV dinner: Mrs. Fearnow's in the yellow can, Wonder bread, and sweetened iced tea.

Bubba Belt: The South, because it has more Bubbas per square mile than anywhere else.

Bubba Magazine: Where it all comes together for Bubbas who can read; lots of laughs, lots of pictures. By Bubbas, for Bubbas.

Buck knife: Fish scaler, fingernail cleaner, and toothpick all in one.

Camaro: Bubba's home may be his castle, but he's the king in his Camaro.

Campfire: Bubba stopped camping out after his son graduated from Scouts, but he still builds a campfire at least once a year. When it's rip-roaring, he pokes it with a stick and moves as the wind shifts, but slow enough so that his long johns and winter coat acquire that smoky campfire smell he likes so much.

Captain's Wafers: Bubba always gets first choice from the Shoney's cracker basket.

Carhartt: Jackets, hats, overalls, pants, and other work clothes that are windproof, barbed-wire-proof, shotgun-pellet-proof. They often pass the Bubba rip-proof test too: no tears after hitting pavement when Bubba, trying to get the last pinch out of a snuff tin, falls out of a pickup truck.

June Carter Cash: Eldest daughter of Maybelle Carter, and, shucks, you know who she is, godmother of Hank Williams Jr. and wife of the Man in Black.

Catfish: Best served with hush puppies and slaw at some great spot like the River Inn in Chattanooga, with a country jukebox, a cold Pabst, and fewer pretensions than John Madden changing his socks.

Chamber music: What Bubba listens to in the bathroom.

Charlie's Angels: The thought of Jill (Farrah Fawcett) behind the wheel of a white '76 Mustang still holds its special place in Bubba's shelf of fond memories. While he could never bring himself to watch *Dynasty*, whenever it was on, Bubba'd ask his wife whether she knew that John Forsythe was the voice of Charlie.

Chaw: "Gotta chaw?" "Red Man, alright?" "Well, I chew Beechnut, but it'll do."

Chili-cheese dog: The undisputed champ of Bubba's diet. What is disputed, though, is whether he prefers the squirt dispenser or the ladle for getting the proportion of chili to liquid cheese just right. Some also heap on onions, relish, and mustard, but Bubba knows that with every condiment in the convenience store piled on, the dog won't fit into its Styrofoam box. How he eats it is never an issue, until someone has to wash the stains out of his favorite T.

Clicker: Bubba was born cable-ready. He's a pro channel surfer, which is why his wife and kids won't watch TV with him anymore.

Coke: Generic for soft drink. As in "Wanna Coke?" "Yeah, gimme one." "What kind?" "Mountain Dew."

Convoy: When Bubba hits the highway headin' for Vacationville, he wants to be in the belly of a convoy, cruising like "a rocket sled on rails." You can bet, too, he's humming the tune to "Convoy" and dreaming of a long and lonesome stretch of Nebraska interstate, even though he's headed south on 95.

Cow tipping: Often practiced by young Bubbas. Instructions: Drink lots of beer at night with buddies, run into a field, and knock down a hapless bovine. Makes a great sound.

Crack: The chink in Bubba's armor, found between the tail of his shirt and the top of his trousers when he bends over.

"Dadgum!": "Goddam!" spelled sideways. Enables Bubba to express his displeasure in mixed company, and without taking the Lord's name in vain.

John Daly: Bubba loves a guy who can drink and drive.

Deer hunting: In this sport the king is the dog driver, who trains his hounds throughout the year and drives them through the weeds during hunting season with manly shouts of "Hiyea! Hiyea!" while cradling a treasured shotgun. The pawns are the standers, who draw positions, then wait for a deer to run by. The sport involves much travel in four-wheel drives, talking on CB radios, and drinking of hot coffee. The whiskey comes later.

Cecil B. DeMille: Any guy who can make a big-budget action movie out of the Bible is okay by Bubba.

Divot: The only ditch-digging Bubba does without pay.

Duck: What Bubba does when he's in a blind with a rookie.

Duct tape: Bubba's dream product. He patches his car seats, winterizes his home, and repairs Junior's basketball—all with duct tape. What he can't understand is why Bubbette won't let him near the broken china.

Dump: What you can call Bubba's favorite restaurant without insulting him.

Dunk: Bubba's best jumping days are behind him. These days a hot mug of coffee and half a dozen cake doughnuts constitutes a slam dunk.

Earthworm: Rain gain.

Easy: How Bubba likes his eggs prepared. He says, "Three o'er easy, Ma'am." Unless, of course, he wants them scrambled, or poached, or soft-boiled, or sunny-side up.

Clint Eastwood: No, dying ain't a good livin'. But, whether he's playing a cowboy or a cop, Clint has lines to kill for. Even though he's heard it at least a thousand times, Bubba still gets a chill out of this one: "You've got to ask

yourself one question: Do I feel lucky? Well, do ya, punk?" Sure.

El Camino: The Chevy El Camino began its reign as Bubba's twofer vehicle (along with Ford's Ranchero) in 1959. To Bubba this proto-model looks like a pick-up-truck version of the Batmobile, minus the turbojet. But most remember the El Camino in its '70s prime: a low-slung Malibu cab with a cargo bed big enough to pitch a small engine block into. The El Camino was phased out in 1987, in case you haven't noticed.

E.T.: Traveled 200,000 light-years for some Reese's Pieces. Bubba can identify.

Everly Brothers: Purveyors of some of the sweetest harmonies to ever come out of Kentucky. Or anyplace else, for that matter. Bubba fell in love to "All I Have to Do Is Dream" and got married to "Let It Be Me."

E-Z Sharpener: The only commercial novaculite in the world is found within 15 miles of Hot Springs, Arkansas. The ultimate Bubba-dad gift idea.

Farmer's blow: *Not* a cut in government crop subsidies. A useful skill for the hanky-less, and like the farmer's almanac, not necessarily just for farmers. Urban Bubbas in the frigid Northeast often horrify passersby with their sidewalk version of this time-tested talent. But beware, learning can require an unpleasant amount of trial and error.

Financial planning: Come Saturday night, if Bubba's got finances, he's got plans. And they actually go to business school to learn that stuff?

Flatt and Scruggs: Finger-pickin' virtuosos, Lester and Earl wrote and played "The Ballad of Jed Clampett." They also played themselves on the *The Beverly Hillbillies.*

Foreplay: Best description of Bubba's golf game. He swats the ball, and yells "Fore!" to warn the folks on the adjacent fairway to run for cover. According to Bubba's own personal rules of etiquette, all's fair if you can find it.

4X4: Where Bubba wears his Yosemite Sam mudflaps.

Fox hunt: No horses are involved in the Bubba version, just—you got it—dogs. Bubbas let their hounds run the fox ragged overnight while they sit around the campfire and do Bubba things.

Redd Foxx: Fred Sanford always promised to marry Nurse Harris but never did, fought with Aunt Esther, and feigned a heart attack every time his 34-year-old son, Lamont, tried to leave home: "I'm coming, Elizabeth. I'm coming." Foxx invented Urban Bubba.

Fry: What Bubba's daughter does at the lake, his son does at White Castle, his wife does to corned-beef hash, and what Bubba baits his hook with.

Gamble: When the needle's on empty, there's still 20 miles to go, and Jack whizzes by the off ramp despite Diane's advice.

Garage (workshop): To Bubba what the kitchen is to Bubbette. In a lifetime, he typically logs more than 23,000 hours—and abandons 345 projects—piddling around here. Most of his time is spent cleaning and reorganizing. He usually stocks canned beer in a mini-fridge and naps on a plastic-covered sofa left over from the '70s. Fortunately, Bubbette accomplishes much more in the kitchen.

General Lee: Bo and Luke Duke's souped-up Dodge Charger. During six years of filming the Dukes totaled 300 General Lees.

Golden Arches: Keep the Ark da Treeumf. As

long as these arches soar over the land of the free and the home of the 69¢ cheeseburger, Bubba will never want for a psychic anchor or a home away from home.

Golf: Area between Texas and Florida where Deep South Bubbas like to fish.

Gotdamdog: Whatever the hound dog does is always funny to Bubba. But when it's the family terrier with a propensity to hump a guest's leg at a backyard cookout, Bubba swats at the dog with his boot and says, "Gotdamdog."

Grits: A good backdrop for salt and butter. Also, what Bubba calls Bubbas he considers beneath him.

Gitar: Fetzer's Uncle Chink says nothing will ruin a young man faster than hanging a gitar on his shoulder.

Gun control: Bubba's idea of gun control is a firm grip. He can knock out the eye of a grasshopper in a green field at 50 yards. If there's a sticker on Bubba's bumper, it's the round badge of either the NRA or the Marine Corps. Funny, they look alike.

Ham radio: In the '70s, Bubba owned a ham radio, basically a powerful CB that allowed him to talk to foreign Bubba-types. The ham bonus: a 50-foot antenna tower in the backyard and secret codes instead of corny CB handles.

Handicap: The number of strokes Bubba gets to deduct from his score when determining whether he and his partner, or their opponents, have to fund the 19th-hole activities.

Hardware store: A daytrip. Bubba's Toys-R-Us.

Hey, Bubba!: Traditional Bubba greeting.

Hockey: Ice, action, blood, beer.

Homegrown tomatoes: A whole different species from the Styrofoam Christmas ornaments you get at the grocery store.

Homer: A man after Bubba's own heart; Bart's father. Best quote: "Mmmmmm, beer."

Home Shopping Channel: Bubba's idea of a shopping spree is his favorite chair, a cold beer, his clicker, and an HSC Bargathon.

Hooters: The waitresses wear orange dresses with logos that feature an owl whose eyes look suspiciously like two breasts. When Bubba goes on a business trip, he always goes to Hooters, where the food is "more than a mouthful."

Hunt: This ol' dog will.

Ibeenmeaninto: Standard Bubba sentence construction, as in "I been meanin' to fix them brakes on the truck..."

In-laws: Bubba Kryptonite.

Instruction manuals: Bubba considers deciphering product literature the same as reading a novel, but more inspirational.

Interstate highways: Bubba-built, Bubba-tested. The American symbol of freedom until the last drop of fossil fuel on the planet goes up in smoke.

Isometric exercise: Bubba in his La-Z-Boy.

Jack: Can mean sour-mash whiskey, money, or enemy, as in "You ain't talking friendly now, Jack."

Jerry Jeff: Texas Bubba musical hero. Classic lines: "It's up against the wall, redneck mother,

mother who has raised her son so well. He's 34 and drinking in a honkytonk, just kickin' hippies' asses and raising hell." Sometimes Bubba even sings along.

Johnson: If weather forecasters, economists, and lovers were as reliable as Bubba's 20-year-old outboard, he wouldn't need to go to heaven when he dies.

Junior Johnson: Essential name in the Bubba cannon. Invented the "power slide" while running moonshine. Arrested by revenuers in 1955—not on a delivery but standing by the still. Went on to win seven Grand National Championships.

George "No Show" Jones: Whiskey-voiced country-music legend who acquired his whiskey voice honestly. Has a problem making it to his own concerts on time, if at all. A run of 50-some missed shows during 1978 and 1979 lead to the nickname.

Khomeini: Still pisses Bubba off.

Kin: Jimmy had Billy; Bill has Roger. You love 'em, you hate 'em, you got 'em.

Evel Knievel: Bubba loved the nasty crashes after the jumps over too many cars. And he had to respect a guy who weathered 433 bone fractures. But Bubba did some parachuting during his army days, and he didn't think floating into a river canyon qualified as much of a stunt.

Krystal Burgers: So small you could eat a dozen. So good you just might. They're the perfect nightcap after a long night drinking beer with the boys. Many's the morning Bubba has woken up to cotton mouth, a pounding head, and 15 or 20 empty Krystal boxes strewn across the floor.

Lab: Has earned his place at Bubba's side. Who else will voluntarily jump into an icy swamp at dawn and fetch—but not eat—his ducks?

Landfill: Where Bubba goes on Saturday after his post-hunting breakfast and before the pre-game football shows. He often takes one of his kids or a Bubba friend to talk to. He backs up right to the very edge of the garbage cliff and pushes over the lawn trimmings or the busted couch that's been in the garage for no less than six months. He points out the broken-winged buzzard hanging out by the tree line and looks for things that he might be able to fix.

Lawn: Bubba's outdoor den, where he keeps the toys Bubbette won't let inside, like his canoe, dirt bike, and jeep trailer.

Lincoln: Carries as much metal as a jet plane, but rides like a snowflake sitting on a cloud.

Lonely Hearts Club ad: Wanted—Good woman, who can cook, sew, clean fish. Must own boat and motor. Send photos of boat and motor.

Loretta Lynn's Ranch: Loretta and her husband, Mooney, have kindly installed an above-ground simulated coal mine and a re-created Loretta birthplace at their Hurricane Mills, Tennessee, estate. Bring your tent, trailer, or pickup camper and set a spell.

Lottery: Bubba's lay-away plan. He lays it out, and away it goes.

Made in the U.S.A.: Bubba likes to wave the flag and march in parades, and sometimes when he really gets carried away he'll bust up a Japanese car with a sledgehammer to make a statement on free trade. Actually, Bubba is fairly open-minded when it comes to other countries. The race for second best is still wide open.

Mailbox post: Principal medium for Bubba's rare but colorful artistic bursts. A few popular styles: welded chain links, upright wagon wheel surrounded by cacti, ten-foot-high "air mail" pole, tractor tire, anchor, plow, anything that requires steel pipe.

Marlin fishing: Several Bubbas get together and charter a sport boat for $800. Out in the Gulf Stream, the captain pursues the mighty blue marlin, a fish that tops out at well over 1,000 pounds, and the mate works the rods and baits the hooks. The Bubbas drink, shoot the bull, eat potted meat and Vienna sausages, and blow grits over the side. Any dead marlins that result are sent to the catfish factory.

Masshole: On the Northern Neck of Virginia, Bubba watermen call the eager tourists "come heres." In Maine, home to at least 70% of New England's Bubbas, the term is "summer people," that is, unless they're from a certain state and the day's haul wasn't too good.

Merle: Bubba Trinity—Haggard, Travis, and Watson.

Mertz: Fred and Ethel.

Mixed emotions: How Bubba feels when his wife says she's leaving him and she's taking the dog.

Moonshine: The best distillers of this home-made corn liquor produce a serum that's as smooth to the tongue as silk. Moonshine (also known as white lightnin', panther's breath, or mountain dew) holds an important place in Bubba history, as moonshine runners in Wilkes County, North Carolina, gave birth to the sport of stock-car racing.

The Mrs.: What Bubba calls his wife, as in "I'll be going to the mall tonight with the Mrs." Use of this term implies a lack of control, a sense that she leads and he is but a pawn. Other interchangeables include "the little lady," "the ol' lady," "mama," and "the woman."

Mr. T: Before he was famous, he was a bouncer. T's the sort of unambiguous guy you want on your side barking "You betta watch out, sucka!" at the guy who danced with your date.

Mud bogging: Racing huge gas-and-oil-guzzling four-wheel-drives through massive pits of mud makes a lot of noise and is a great occasion for beer drinking.

NASCAR: Noise. Action. Six pack. Cooler. Asphalt. Rubber.

Naugahyde: Naugs come in colors cows never dreamed of.

Hal Needham: Stunt coordinator and director of *Smokey and the Bandit* and *Cannonball Run.* Bubbas like car crashes, and nobody has crashed more than Hal.

Nuclear power plants: They always seem to build them a half-mile from Bubba's home. The constant hum is a mite vexing, but the cucumbers and snaps in the garden just keep getting bigger and better.

No. 2: Performed out of doors, this is a Bubba rite of passage requiring an engineer's eye for angles and a botanist's knowledge of leaves that don't make you itch. Bubba never calls it No. 2.

Okra: Boiled, it has the consistency of milkweed marinated in Elmer's glue. Sliced and fried, which is about the only way Bubba will eat it, okra is up there with homegrown tomatoes.

Onliest: The way Bubba emphasizes the singular, as in "Richard Petty is the onliest King of stock-car racing."

Opossum: The great roadside casualty of Bubba

America. A opossum could find a way to get run over by a pickup truck parked in a driveway.

Orlando: Some may call its amusement parks, magic kingdoms, resource-sapping water rides and strip motels an environmental catastrophe; Bubba calls it the most fun per acre in America.

Pabst Blue Ribbon: Bubba likes PBR for the same reasons he liked peanut butter and jelly on Wonder bread when he was a kid: Both satisfy his primal needs in a simple, unflashy way. And he never got too full on just one.

Dolly Parton: Bubba's been planning to take the family to Dollywood ever since he can remember. He can't wait to visit Dolly's Dressing

Room. He still keeps that *Playboy* with her on the cover stashed under the mattress—even though it's only an interview.

Patsy: Bubba is crazy about Patsy. He just falls to pieces every time he hears her voice.

Pellet gun: Training wheels for junior Bubba hunters, who are often caught taking aim at the neighbor's cat.

Penthouse: Why Bubba has gone to the same barber for 20 years.

Petty: The crown has passed from granddad Lee, who won the first Daytona 500, to father Richard, the King himself, to son Kyle, who got the benefits of the bloodline. They teach Di and Charles a thing or two about heritage.

Pickled eggs: The more pink, the more pickled. Cheaper by the gallon.

Planetary housing: Not Bubba's solution to the homeless problem. Encases gearing between the axle and the wheels of a truck.

Plug: As in tobacco. When Raymond says, "Earl,

hand me that plug," he isn't about to stick something into a socket. He wants a chew.

Price Club: Finding out that you made the cut for membership is only half the fun. The other half is loading a hand truck with 5-gallon vats of pickles and enough Twinkies to last two generations. Bubba loves a place where he can buy cases of beer, a 20-pound sack of peanuts, and a large-screen T.V. all at once.

Quick: As in "Mary Lou's quick as small-town gossip."

Quick lunch: Vinyl-top stools, Hobart deep fryer, plenty of stainless, and friendly faces.

Quid: Quid pro huh? In Bubbadom it's another word for "chaw."

Quitting Time: And Quitting Time Light. Cheaper than Bud, better than generic. Boss says, "It's quitting time!"

Range balls: Take some with you on the course. The handy red stripe is perfect for lining up your club face. They don't travel as far as a Titleist, which is actually a good thing when half your shots precede a walk in the woods. Great for water holes.

Rear end: Bubba gets distracted by a pretty thing walking down the street. He locks eyes, then brakes, then bumpers. It doesn't hurt what he's driving but puts a real humdinger in someone else's rear end.

Red-eye: For Bubba this one means many things, none of which is the late-night flight

from L.A. to New York. On Sunday morning, it's gravy, or beer and tomato juice (when a whole beer just won't set). The night before, it was seeing inside the crack of a moon when a car of rowdy teenagers drove by.

Redman: Bubba supports the Braves, the Chiefs and the 'Skins in their choices of name. And doggone if Bubba's gonna chew "Native American Man."

Retire: What Bubba does when the humus finally starts to rot the rubber of his garden planters.

Burt Reynolds: Throws a tight spiral, shoots a mean bow, posed nude for Cosmoplitan, once risked his life to transport a truckload of beer across a state line; and he's Loni's husband. Bubba Mensch.

Rome: "When in Rome, Bubba does as he does at home." Bub knows his roots and sticks to it.

Roseanne: Feistiest Bubbette, Barr none.

Arnold Schwarzenegger: Some actors ask to keep antiques or costumes as souvenirs from their movies. Arnold asks for giant pieces of military hardware. He has Bubba priorities.

Scrimshaw: An art form belonging exclusively to Bubba. The best artisans create entire landscapes on the handles of a knife. Next time you hear someone talk about some modern art being "cutting-edge," tell them your art comes with a 12-inch, stainless-steel blade.

See a man...: Take a pee, as in "Sorry, Bubba, but I'll be right back. I gotta see a man about a horse."

Shoes: Played a couple of nights a week with a few close friends. Best to play doubles to avoid walking back and forth.

Sign shooting: Best practiced at night while drinking with friends in a pickup truck. The trick is to track down a stationary highway sign and blow it away using a shotgun loaded with buckshot. Then roar off before the cops catch you. In some rural pockets, it's hard to find a sign that hasn't been wounded.

Skid marks: Too fast to slow down or too slow to pull 'em down.

Smells: When the family dog is not around, Bubba gets blamed for any smell this side of Chanel No. 9. While on the way to the grocery store, the Bubbeasties in the backseat cry in unison, "DAAADDY! Gross!" Even in winter, the kids and the Mrs. roll down all the windows.

Snap-On Tools: Excellent source of calendars.

Snow skiing: Bubba tried skiing *once*, but he draws the line at seeing a psychiatrist.

S.O.S.: Cream chipped beef on toast, otherwise known as shit on a shingle.

South of the Border: Disney World substitute after a lean year.

Spit: Universal solvent.

Spork: The plastic spoon-fork for eating mashed potatoes at KFC. Lick it clean and have some chocolate pudding.

Straight shooter: Drinking bourbon or gin straight out of the bottle, chased by a gulp of soda. Whiskey and Sun-drop is a popular combo in some parts. Bubbas with stomach problems chase their whiskey with liver pudding.

Surday (or Sardy): The day before Sunday.

Sushi: Fish bait.

Tank top: If Michael Dukakis had looked as comfortable in one as Bubba does on the boardwalk at Myrtle Beach, he might have won....Well, nah.

Tellin' lies: Bubba never lies, but sometimes he *tells* lies—mostly on fishing boats, around campfires, in front of a wood stove, or in a barber shop.

Thanksgiving: Bubba's favorite holiday—no gifts, lots of chow, football.

Toothpicks: Bubba uses them in public places without embarrassment. Toothpicks dance on the lip for hours. Similarly, nail clippers come to work, and Bubbette can brush her hair and preen at a table in the Food Court.

Dick Trickle: 1989 NASCAR Rookie of the Year. Bubba loves to talk about this guy's stats, his brilliant future, his....Okay, okay, Bubba likes to say his name and belly laugh.

Trophy shop: Frequented by Moose and Elk clubbers, bass-tournament organizers, Little League coaches, regional Scout administrators, and other bred-in-the-bone Bubbas. Bubba's dream: to quit the daily grind and open his own.

Trucks and Tractor Power: The Nashville Network's half hour of power—featuring monster trucks, mud bogs, and mechanical tugs-of-war—seen by 432,000 households at a crack.

$250: Annual cost to be a "Top Alcohol Funny Car Patron" at the "Big Daddy" Don Garlits Museum of Drag Racing and International Drag Racing Hall of Fame. Includes newsletter, annual passes, a 15% gift-shop discount, MODR cap and lapel pin, and a window decal.

Ugly: As in "Joo make him pay?" "Yessir, I got on him like ugly on an ape."

Un-: For better or for worse, Bubba is unabashed, unadorned, unaffected, unblinking, uncompromising, and at times uncommunicative. But Bubba usually isn't unarmed.

Vanity plates: Bubba gets a kick out of having things personalized—coffee mugs, gun cases, bowling shirts, and golf-club head covers. And he loves to advertise his passions on his plates. Some favorites: IM4GOLF, DEERHNTR, BUCKFVR, BVRFVR, 2HOT4U, XLR8, AWESUM, MUDDIN.

VCR: It was a matter of pride to Bubba that he could work his. When the five hundred cable channels finally come through, Bubba will make a special trip to the landfill to give his VCR a proper burial.

Velcro: God's own gift to Bubba comfort. Just loosen that baby up an inch or so and pass the hush puppies. Bubba only wishes they'd had Velcro back when his daddy was around; a Velcro whuppin' would have beat a belt whuppin' any day of the week.

Velour: The La-Z-Boy of comfort wear.

Velveeta: The clue to the *Jeopardy* question "What goes perfect on a sandwich between the bologna and the onions?"

Velvet Elvis: Soft corn.

Victoria's Secret Catalog: The best thing that's happened to Bubba since Bubbette found and tossed his magazine stash. And it's free.

Violin: A fiddle played by a foreign guy.

Virgil: Teller of classic tales—fishing tales, that is. You know, Virgil Ward.

Virginia: She's been married five times to four men. She places $2 bets, not big ones. She fishes with live minnows and has a bust of Elvis. Bill's unimpeachable claim to Bubbahood.

Vittles: All food that is good, simple, and unpretentious. If it comes with a side order of cole slaw, it's vittles. If it comes with mango pine nut chutney, it ain't.

Volunteer fire department: Redundant in Bub-
baville. Count him in.

Waffle House: The Interstate wouldn't be the
same without the Waffle House. Bubba families like the chain best because the jukeboxes
have songs about how great Waffle Houses are.
While the waitresses hate the songs, gems like
the "Waffle Doo-Wop" are tonic to the burnt-
out, traveling Bubba family.

Watermelon: The second most famous thing to
come out of Hope, Arkansas, where they hold
a festival for the fruit every August. When they
say they grow 'em big and round in Hope, they
don't just mean presidents.

WD-40: What duct tape is to mending, WD-40
is to lubrication.

Wreck: Why Bubba never trades in his car.

Wild man: An affectionate term for male friends. As in "Whaddya say, wild man?"

Wonder bread: Still the best side dish with barbecue, and the only choice for a decent grilled cheese. It'll be around long after those multi-grain pebble loaves have stopped blocking the national digestive system. Wonder bread isn't much on fiber, but they throw in enough essential vitamins so that one sandwich will inoculate you against five or six diseases.

X-lent: Bubba shorthand for good news.

Xmas: Why Bubba loves the Home Shopping Channel.

X ray: What Bubbette makes Bubba get six months after a horse throws him onto a pile of rocks. He'll have to be tricked into going even then. They always come out positive.

Xtra sauce?: Yes, please.

XX: Home brew used by Granny to fire up the Clampett-mobile.

Yellow: The traffic-light color that means Bubba should step on it.

Yessir: What the gas-station Bubba-attendant answers when you tell him the route you're taking to where you think you're going.

Yesterday: Always somehow just a little bit better than today. Country music was invented to never let us forget that fact.

Yoo Hoo: Bubba's favorite cold beverage other than beer.

Zactlies: An ailment that afflicts Bubba after a night of carousing. He wakes up the next day and discovers that his mouth tastes zactly like his fish cooler after a long day in the sun.

Zapper: Bubba's summertime backyard scud-buster.

Zipperhead: An uncouth Bubba's hairstyle, divvied down the middle. Not by a comb but by gravity. This no-maintenance coif never goes out of style, because it never was *in* style. Advantage: looks the same clean or greasy. Also known as the butt-cut in some circles.

Spinnin' a Windy

Bubba's always been one to call a bucket a bucket. But no one ever said he was afraid to spice up his metaphors. Here are a few twists on his favorite conversation pieces.

Lying

While shootin' the bull over a six-pack, Bubba might remark that perhaps Ricky's pole-bustin' fish story was a bit farfetched. But he won't.

He'll say that Ricky just sawed off a whopper or spun a windy. He could even say that Ricky sure stretched the blanket on that one.

Looks

Bubba's wife may be so scarce-hipped she could take a bath in a gun barrel, but the effects of ball games and finger food have made Bubba fat as a town cow. Still, Bubba doesn't even cast a shadow beside Uncle Eddie, who's so big that when he hauls ass, he has to make two trips.

You can bet that on prom night, Bubba's son, Junior, will be decked out from stem to gudgeon. He'd like to brag that his date's a real lolliper (looker). As it turns out, sorry to say, she fell out of the ugly tree and hit every branch on the way down. Junior's best friend says he wouldn't take her to a dog fight—even if she had a chance to win.

Poverty

By nature, Bubba wants to give his family the best, and he usually avoids having to suck the hind tit. But he does have some friends who live in houses so small they have to go outside to change their minds. Jimmy Lee on Rte. 5 is so poor he can't even pay attention. Back in Depression times, Bubba's parents said their backs could split raindrops. When talking about his folks now, Bubba says they were as broke as the Ten Commandments.

Scrappin'

Bubba does his best to avoid a fight, but he'll push his way through a crowd to watch a good one. He remembers when Slick went into the local bar acting like he'd just hung the moon. Hoss, already in a bad mood and taking none of that, decided to raise some sand. When Slick spilled his beer on Hoss's boot, Hoss stepped back and put his big fist into Slick's surprised face—upped his trotters in one punch. But before the two could really tear off a strip, the bartender yanked them apart. Otherwise, Hoss would've cleaned Slick's plow.

Stupidity

Bubba may be dumb, but he ain't stupid. That's not to say that all his friends are smarter than a barrel of hair. His buddy Booger's a heck of a handyman, but if brains were dynamite, he couldn't blow his own nose.

Earl takes the trophy for being a few bricks shy of a full load. He's been called stupid in so many ways, Bubba can't remember the half of them: Earl's half a bubble off plumb, as close to smart as a frog is to hair. He couldn't drive nails in a snow bank or kick-start a can opener. He don't know "come 'ere" from "sic 'em." Earl don't even know straight up from apple butter.

Where Bubba's From Folks Understand Him

Sometimes Bubba is hard to understand, even to other Bubbas. It may be because he lost his teeth a long time ago or because he has a mouthful of food or tobacco, or just that where Bubba is from everybody else can understand him. In any case, here are some commonly mistaken terms:

If you think Bubba said: Bordeaux, as in the wine that completes a good filet mignon dinner. **He probably said:** Bondo, as in the dominant color of his Fury.

If you think Bubba said: Art deco, as in the fashionable Manhattan interior. **He probably said:** AC Delco, as in the car-parts company whose Chuck Yeager commercials he likes.

If you think Bubba said: Private jeweler, as in for that special Christmas gift. **He probably said:** Playmate cooler, as in the lunch box that doubles as his six-pack suitcase.

If you think Bubba said: Hermes ties, as in what the best dressed execs wear. **He probably said:** Moon Pies, as in what there's no beatin' for eatin' on long car trips.

If you think Bubba said: Eliot's *Waste Land*, as in the piece de resistance of the Lost Generation. **He probably said:** Elvis's Graceland, as in the Memphis Mecca.

If you think Bubba said: Belair, as in the preferred West Coast residence. **He probably said:** Belair, as in the classic showcase for a 327-horsepower engine.

If you think Bubba said: Roast duck, as in *à l'orange*. **He probably said:** Monster truck, as in major mudmobile that kicks ass and makes flames.

Cussin', Kiddin', and Junior's Toys

Ten Bubba Expletives
(fit for public consumption)

Bubba don't curse. Well, he does, actually. But rarely in front of somebody else's children.

1. Shucks!
2. Dag nabbit!
3. Son of a biscuit eater!
4. Good goobity goo!
5. For the love of Pete!
6. Flapdoodle!
7. Corn my pone!
8. Jeeminy!
9. Fish sticks!
10. Scrapple!

Ten Most Common Characters in Bubba's Favorite Jokes

1. State troopers
2. Talking dogs
3. Man from Nantucket
4. Bartenders
5. Gas-meter readers
6. Preachers
7. God
8. Drunk guys
9. Golfers
10. Magic fish

Five Toys Found in Li'l Bubbette's Room

1. The cat
2. Band-Aids
3. Scissors
4. Bald Barbie (see No. 3)
5. Golf bag ("Barbie's Action Cave")

Ten Toys Found in Junior's Room

1. Tonka truck
2. Dried-up frog
3. Dismantled radio
4. Rubber insects
5. G.I. Joe with with Kung Fu Grip
6. Woolly Willie
7. Matches
8. BB gun
9. Spud gun
10. Real gun

Ten Things Found on Bubba's Head*

1. Gimme cap
2. Straw hat
3. Cowboy hat
4. Cap with dual beer holders, straws leading to mouth
5. Pith helmet
6. Lamp shade
7. Child-size birthday-party hat
8. Hard hat
9. Empty 12-pack
10. Burger King crown

* Note the absence of comb-overs or any synthetic hair substitutes.

Ten Places You *Won't* Find Bubba

1. Shoppers Anonymous 12-step meeting
2. The opera
3. Spandex 'N' Things
4. A Richard Simmons video
5. The *Donahue* studio audience
6. Revco's tampon aisle
7. The library
8. Saks Fifth Avenue
9. A sushi bar
10. France

Is Your Passport Stamped "Bubba"?

NO: You pass through customs at Calais, France, after crossing the English Channel from Dover. You enjoy wonderful food in Calais and think the French are neat.

YES: You pass through customs at Calais, Maine, after crossing the St. Croix River from New Brunswick. That's KALL-us, not Kal-LAY. You find so-so food, but some great hardware stores.

NO: Your summer rental home in the Hamptons, Long Island, features a hot tub, cedar deck, and ocean views.

YES: Your motel room in Hampton Beach, N.H., features somewhat clean linen, a yellow spot on the wall shaped like Idaho, and views of Bubba families sunning themselves like wildebeests at the pool.

NO: At a Monte Carlo casino you hit 33 black on the roulette wheel and walk away with $4,000. You celebrate with a bottle of Dom.

YES: On the boardwalk at Virginia Beach you find an unclaimed lottery ticket good for $25. You buy a tank top and a Mountain Dew.

NO: On a transatlantic flight, the first-class attendant graciously offers to hang your designer bag in the forward coat compartment.
YES: On a bus trip to Paramus, New Jersey, the driver heaves your duffel bag into the baggage bin, snarls, and says, "Whaddaya got in there, bricks?"

NO: Travel Nightmare: Heathrow is completely socked in with fog, you're flight's been canceled, and the hotel where the airline put you up has a wine list that you'd charitably describe as subpar.
YES: Travel Nightmare: The fan belt on your K Car snaps along I-95 and you roll to a stop next to the biggest outlet mall you've ever seen. The service stations are closed, but the outlet mall is open 24 hours. The last you see of your wife, she's disappearing into a store called Bathroom Fixture World.

NO: Feeling the need to expand your mind while on vacation, you hire a private boat and guide for a tour of the Galàpagos Islands, where you commune with ancient turtles and ponder your place in the evolutionary chain.
YES: All the worldly culture you need is encompassed by two words: Epcot Center.

BubbaMaster Quiz

If you scored above a 150 on the Basic Bubba Quiz, you qualified to take the BubbaMaster examination. No cheating.

1. *Allan Kulwicki won NASCAR's Winston Cup points championship in 1992. Who sponsored his race car?*

    a. Pooter's

    b. Cooter's

    c. Amazoy Zoysia Grass

    d. Hooter's

2. *Who is the King of Stock Car Racing, what was his car number, and how many races did he win in his career?*

    a. Darrell Waltrip; 34; 2,222

    b. Richard Petty; 43; 200

    c. Darrin Stephens; 66; 2,000

    d. Amerigo Vespucci; 00; 20

3. *What is your favorite brand of chewing tobacco?*

    a. I don't chew   c. I don't know

    b. Copenhagen   d. None of the
                                           above

4. *Where is Elvis buried?*

    a. Memphis   c. Graceville

    b. Spaceland, U.S.A.   d. In a graveyard

5. *What is the name of Hank Williams's band?*
   a. The Bocephi
   b. The Long Goners
   c. The Drifting Cowboys
   d. The Goodbye Mama Band

6. *If Bubba is eating escargot, he will be singing*
   a. "Dixie"
   b. "Love Me Tender"
   c. "Rock of Ages"
   d. "Amazing Grace"

7. *Which is the most un-Bubbalike type of fishing?*
   a. Fly-fishing
   b. Jug-fishing
   c. Fishing with a cane pole
   d. Fishing with dynamite

8. *Which of the following was Elvis Presley's first record label?*
   a. RCA
   b. Def Jam
   c. I.R.S.
   d. Sun

9. *Which of the following names has Hulk Hogan used in his career?*
   a. Whitey
   b. Terry "The Hulk" Boulder
   c. Sterling Golden

d. Thunder Lips

e. All of the above

10. *Your prize coondog, Flash, dies. What do you do with his remains?*

    a. Donate them to animal science

    b. Stuff and mount them

    c. Pack the pickup with dry ice and drive them to Tuscumbia, Alabama

    d. Bury them out back

BubbaMaster Quiz Answers

1-d. Hooter's, where the waitresses are like pancakes—stacked.

2-b. Richard Petty; 43; 200. If you missed this one, go back and repeat the first quiz.

3-d. Choosing "I don't know" or "I don't chew" is a bad sign. Chewing is a Bubba social skill much like knowing which fork to use and how to play bridge are in other social circles. Discussing the merits of chewing tobacco brands is a polite way to make small talk and a conversational ice breaker at Bubba social events. If you chose **b.**, Copenhagen, your bluff failed; Copenhagen is snuff.

4. Trick question. If you chose Memphis—or anywhere else, for that matter—you're wrong. Elvis ain't dead.

5-c. The Drifting Cowboys. That's why they had the "Long Gone Lonesome Blues."

6. Another trick question. Bubba knows better than to eat snails. Score 10 only if you refused to answer. But give yourself 5 if you answered. Some Bubbas just can't resist these tunes.

7-a. Fly-fishing. The effort exerted and how much Bubba likes that style of fishing are inversely proportional. Besides, have you ever tried to hold a fish fry with the catch from one day's worth of fly-fishing?

8-d. Sun. This is a must-know question. If you got it wrong the rest of the quiz is not valid.

9-e. Hulk, known as Whitey in high school, used his superlative Bubba work ethic to mountain muscles on his 6'6" frame. Wrestling manager Classy Freddie Blassie introduced Hulk to the World Wrestling Federation in 1979. The rest is neck-wrenching history.

10-c. Tuscumbia is home to the Key Underwood Memorial Coondog Graveyard, which accepts only true-blood hounds. No Labs.

Scoring

Give yourself 10 points for each correct answer. Add up your total. *Extra credit: Add 5 points to your score if your obituary will read, "_____ was a member of the Price Club."*

Your grade

If you scored under **50 points**, go back and take the Basic Bubba Quiz over again; you must have gotten lucky or cheated the first time. If you scored under **75 points**, listen to Jerry Jeff Walker's *Viva Terlingua* every day for two weeks and attend a pig pickin', then try again. **Over 85**? Get yourself a new bass boat and take a two-week vacation. Tell your boss we said so. You earned it.

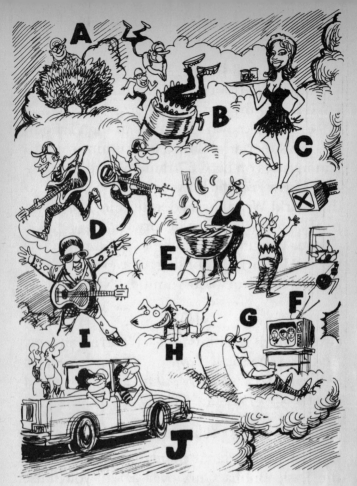

Bubba Heaven

A. An outdoor urinal **B.** The bottomless keg **C.** Vanna as waitress **D.** A guitar that magically allows you to play like Chuck Berry **E.** A truly no-stick grill top **F.** Auto-score bowling **G.** The All-Stooges Network **H.** A flea collar that really works **I.** Elvis as your next-door neighbor **J.** Excellent parking

Bubba Magazine Staff

Editors **Dean King**, **Jessica King**, **Logan Ward**, and **Greg "Grease" Easley** were all born and raised in the Bubba Belt but migrated to New York to find work. In addition to *Bubba Magazine*, they write and edit *The Southern Farmer's Almanac* and the *Penny Pincher's Almanac*.

Art director **Paul Hebert** formerly did the same for *National Review*. Illustrator **Bay Rigby**, a former *New York Post* political cartoonist, is a "Bubber" from Down Under.

Contributors

Wall Street Bubba **Tayloe Dameron**, originally from Virginia, is an old dipping buddy of the editor's.

Bill "Wombat" Martin, originally from Florida, writes for *In Living Color* in Hollywood.

Fetzer Mills lives in North Carolina, chews Red Man, and drives a pickup truck.

Free-lance writer **Garland Pollard IV** lives in Virginia.

John Railey lives in North Carolina and writes for the *High Point Enterprise*.

When he's not in Baltimore, **Allen "Alvis" Randolph** grows sideburns in New York.

Charlie Slack, a Yankee Bubba who reverse-migrated south, is a staff writer for the *Richmond Times-Dispatch*.

Vince Staten is the author of *Real Barbecue* and *Can You Trust a Tomato in January?* He lives in Kentucky.